Especially for

From

Date

BARBOUR BOOKS

An Imprint of Barbour Publishing, Inc.

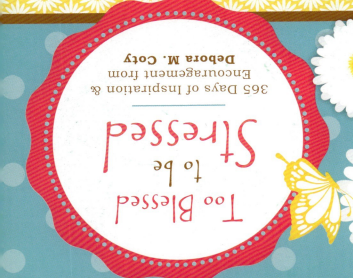

Too Blessed to be Stressed

365 Days of Inspiration &
Encouragement from
Debora M. Coty

ISBN 978-1-68322-399-3

Published by Barbour Books, an imprint of Barbour Publishing, Inc., 1810 Barbour Drive, Uhrichsville, Ohio 44683, www.barbourbooks.com

Our mission is to inspire the world with the life-changing message of the Bible.

Printed in China.

January 1

Take a deep breath.
Close your eyes.
Exhale slowly.
There.
You've just taken the first
step in stress reduction.

January 2

Good judgment comes
from bad experiences
and a lot of that comes
from bad judgment.

UNKNOWN

January 3

TIME TO LOL!

I knew it was time to address
my stress issues when my growl
grew louder than the dog's,
and my fam tactfully suggested
I get a rabies shot.

January 4

God will never let you down.

1 Corinthians 10:13 msg

January 5

Pressure creates both
diamonds and volcanoes.

January 6

Let a few things go. Tomorrow,
release a few more.
In time, those tasks will
quit nagging at you,
and you'll literally feel the
stress rocks in your stomach
disintegrate into dust!

January 7

When we live life in a hurry,
we end up weary . . . in a hurry.

KERI WYATT KENT

January 8

The LORD said, "I will go with you and give you peace."

EXODUS 33:14 CEV

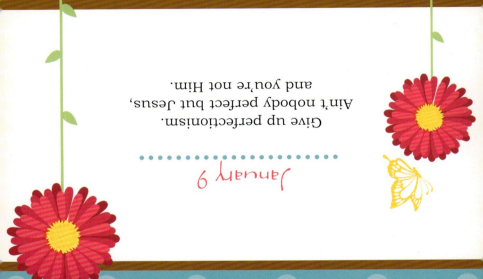

January 9

Give up perfectionism.
Ain't nobody perfect but Jesus,
and you're not Him.

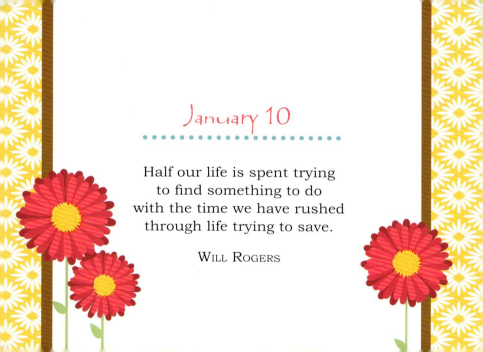

January 10

Half our life is spent trying
to find something to do
with the time we have rushed
through life trying to save.

WILL ROGERS

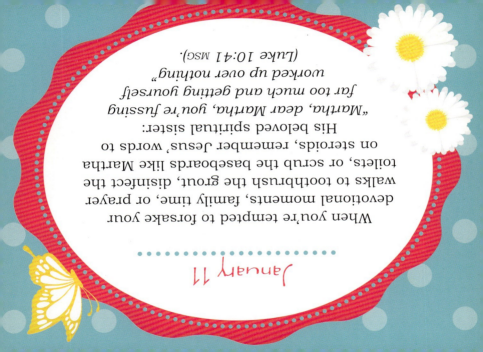

January 11

When you're tempted to forsake your devotional moments, family time, or prayer walks to toothbrush the grout, disinfect the toilets, or scrub the baseboards like Martha on steroids, remember Jesus' words to His beloved spiritual sister:

"Martha, dear Martha, you're fussing far too much and getting yourself worked up over nothing" (Luke 10:41 MSG).

January 12

"The joy of the LORD is your strength."

NEHEMIAH 8:10 NIV

January 13

Positive self-talk is a *huge* part of everyday stress management. By choosing an upbeat attitude, our outlook becomes much more optimistic and consequently much less stress producing.

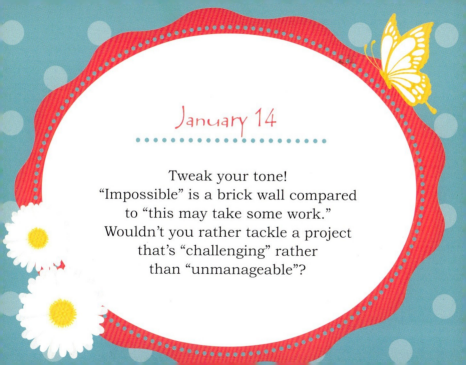

January 14

Tweak your tone!
"Impossible" is a brick wall compared
to "this may take some work."
Wouldn't you rather tackle a project
that's "challenging" rather
than "unmanageable"?

January 15

Unless you're the reigning world champion, there will always be someone better than you at a specific skill. So what? You don't need another tiara.

January 16

Let all things be done decently and in order.

1 Corinthians 14:40 KJV

January 17

Rearrange the following priorities in order of importance to you: "me" time, family, faith, work, success, appearance, relationships, schedules. On which three do you spend the most time?

January 18

· ·

Act positively to actually become
positive. In other words, putting on a
happy-face mask truly makes
us *feel* happier!

January 19

Memorize Philippians 4:13.
Repeat frequently.
Trust God, and act on it!

*I can do everything through
Christ, who gives me strength.*
PHILIPPIANS 4:13 NLT

January 20

When we allow negative self-talk,
we're not only limiting ourselves,
but also limiting our God—the Creator
of the universe—the One who is
ready to fill us with expectancy
and hope and potential.

January 21

Words are powerful.
They have the ability to
change our perception
of our own abilities
from *limited* to *limitless*.

January 22

Whether you think you can
or think you can't—you are right.

HENRY FORD

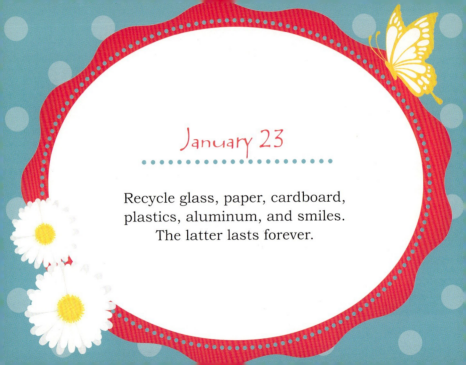

January 23

Recycle glass, paper, cardboard,
plastics, aluminum, and smiles.
The latter lasts forever.

January 24

If our minds are ruled by our desires, we will die. But if our minds are ruled by the Spirit, we will have life and peace.

ROMANS 8:6 CEV

January 25

Keep your eyes on Jesus. . . . Remember, it's His power and His presence that ultimately heal. God really does do broken-heart surgery.

January 26

The next time you feel like yelling,
"Stick a toothpick in me; I'm done!"
remember that although our "oven"
days are difficult—often painful—
those are the times we grow
and mature in our faith.

January 27

Be your own BFF! Speak to yourself
like you would your very best friend.
Make it a point to be encouraging,
uplifting, affirming, light,
and humorous (you'll listen better!).

January 28

[Jesus] said, "Martha, dear Martha,
you're fussing far too much
and getting yourself worked
up over nothing."

LUKE 10:41 MSG

January 29

· ·

Do everything in moderation,
including moderation.

BEN FRANKLIN

January 30

Beauty is always there;
we just don't see it when our
eyes are focused on our to-do lists.

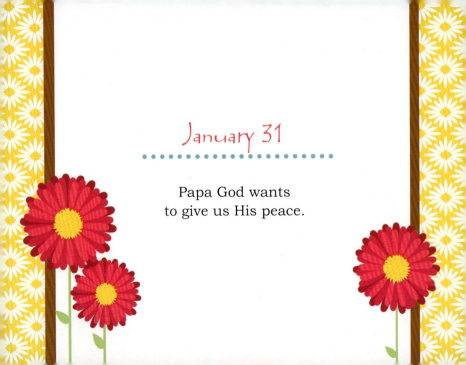

January 31

· ·

Papa God wants
to give us His peace.

February 1

*Fix your thoughts on what is true,
and honorable, and right, and pure,
and lovely, and admirable. Think about things
that are excellent and worthy of praise.*

PHILIPPIANS 4:8 NLT

February 2

. . . .

TIME TO LOL!

Housekeeping is a perpetual lesson
in futility. Cleaning an occupied
house is like combing your
hair in a hurricane.

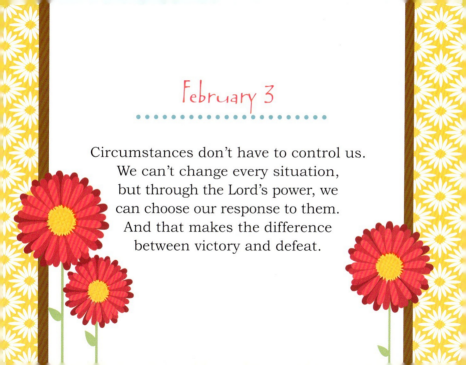

February 3

Circumstances don't have to control us.
We can't change every situation,
but through the Lord's power, we
can choose our response to them.
And that makes the difference
between victory and defeat.

February 4

Communicate with Papa God
every day in every way.
Pray as if your life depends
on it—because it does!

February 5

· ·

Whatever you do in word or deed,
do all in the name of the Lord.

COLOSSIANS 3:17 NASB

February 6

· · · · · · · · · · · · · · · · · · · ·

Grasp every opportunity to recognize
God's fingerprints in the details
of your everyday life.

February 7

There's never enough time to
do all the nothing you want.

BILL WATTERSON, *CALVIN AND HOBBES*

February 8

Healing is a dollar-off coupon,
not a blowout sale. It's an incremental
process. Step by tiny step, just keep
moving in the right direction, and
eventually you'll get there. You will!

February 9

· ·

Yes, my soul, find rest in God;
my hope comes from him.

PSALM 62:5 NIV

February 10

Think about a recent time when you
faced devastating, unexpected loss.
How did you deal with it?
Have you come to the conclusion
that you're too blessed to be stressed?

February 11

How can we turn off the fret faucet?
When the mental-obsession recorder
hits Replay for the tenth time, lay
your problems at the foot of the cross.
Jesus will take them off your hands.

February 12

TIME TO LOL!

Distraction is your friend.
Positive input reduces negative
output. You can't bite your nails
while scrubbing the linoleum.

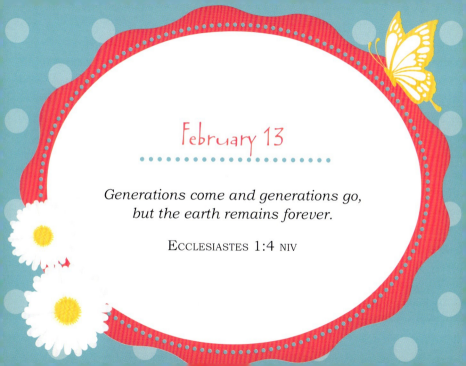

February 13

*Generations come and generations go,
but the earth remains forever.*

ECCLESIASTES 1:4 NIV

February 14

The joy of the Lord brings splashes
of color into our black-and-white world.

February 15

"Be anxious for nothing" takes on new meaning when you grasp the fact that anxiety does absolutely nothing for you.

February 16

Every evening I turn
my worries over to God.
He's going to be
up all night anyway.

MARY C. CROWLEY

February 17

He has never let you down,
never looked the other way when you
were being kicked around. He has never
wandered off to do his own thing;
he has been right there, listening.

PSALM 22:24 MSG

February 18

No matter how organized you are,
something will eventually go awry.
Don't freak. Expect it.
Take control of your attitude
so that your attitude doesn't
take control of you.

February 19

· ·

True strength lies in submission,
which permits one to dedicate
his life, through devotion,
to something beyond himself.

HENRY MILLER

February 20

Today, read Psalm 4 (it's short).
How can we, like David,
find peace in our distress?

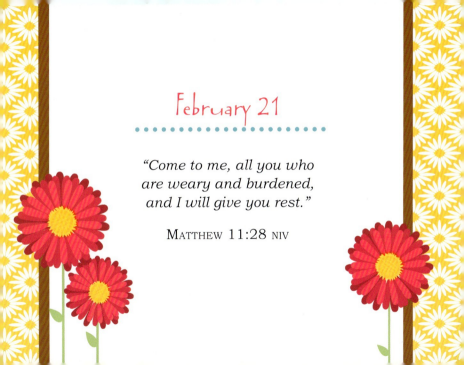

February 21

*"Come to me, all you who
are weary and burdened,
and I will give you rest."*

MATTHEW 11:28 NIV

February 22

There's hope for us, sisters!
You and I can be Cinderella!
Through Papa God's power working
within us, we can transform into a new,
improved version of ourselves beyond
our most extravagant imaginings.

February 23

The sun hasn't disappeared just because
it's temporarily obscured by clouds.
Sometimes those silver linings are
just a belly laugh away.

February 24

What makes you laugh?
A roly-poly puppy? Funny movies?
A favorite comedian? So when was
the last time you set yourself
up for a good belly laugh?

February 25

*Everyone born of God
overcomes the world.*

1 John 5:4 niv

February 26

· ·

TIME TO LOL!

Nature abhors a vacuum.
And so do I.

ANNE GIBBONS

February 27

Humor is God's weapon against worry, anxiety, and fear. It's a powerful salve for the skinned knees of the spirit—healing, revitalizing, protecting us against toxic infections like bitterness, defeat, or depression.

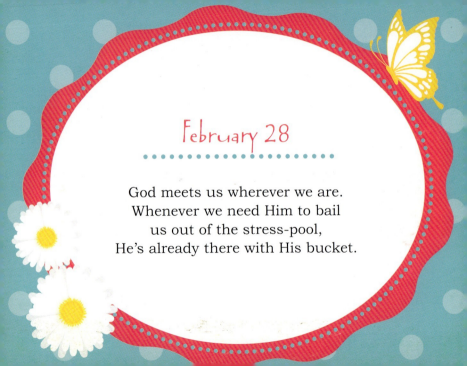

February 28

God meets us wherever we are.
Whenever we need Him to bail
us out of the stress-pool,
He's already there with His bucket.

March 1

Our purpose is to please God, not people.

1 THESSALONIANS 2:4 NLT

March 2

· ·

There is no peace in striving
with your own strength to hold
on to what you may lose.

RUBYE GOODLETT

March 3

· · · · · · · · · · · · · · · · · · · ·

TIME TO LOL!

Swallow your pride occasionally;
it's nonfattening!

UNKNOWN

March 4

• •

TIME TO LOL!

Consciousness is simply
that annoying time between naps.

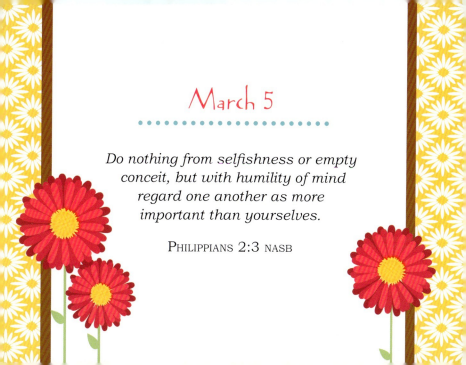

March 5

· ·

*Do nothing from selfishness or empty
conceit, but with humility of mind
regard one another as more
important than yourselves.*

PHILIPPIANS 2:3 NASB

March 6

When you're totally dependent on
God's grace, He never lets you down.

March 7

Lord, please chill my internal inferno
and help me not to have an "ity" day.
You know, an uppity day in which I
demonstrate, in no particular order,
density, banality, crudity, calamity,
stupidity, disunity, ferocity, futility, audacity,
and especially insanity. And thank You
for Your gracious generosity. Amen.

March 8

TIME TO LOL!

My soul's had enough chicken soup,
thank you. Now it needs a little
stimulation; you know—
a choc-tastic attitude adjustment,
mocha milkshake for
the mind, chinning up with
chocolate chunks. . .

March 9

. . . .

*"Who of you by worrying can
add a single hour to your life?
Since you cannot do this very little thing,
why do you worry about the rest?"*

LUKE 12:25–26 NIV

March 10

TIME TO LOL!

My newest political agenda is to petition
Congress to legislate a daily siesta.
We could close all businesses from 1 to
3 p.m., curl up on mats like kindergartners
(after mandatory cookies and milk,
of course), catch some z's, and become a
gentler and kinder nation because of it.

March 11

Happy naps are little slices of heaven
that revive our energy, clarity, and
motivation, our front line of defense
against temperament-raging fatigue,
which results in acute nastiness.

March 12

Those who loved you and were helped
by you will remember you when
forget-me-nots have withered.
Carve your name on hearts, not marble.

CHARLES SPURGEON

March 13

· ·

For God is not a God
of disorder but of peace.

1 CORINTHIANS 14:33 NIV

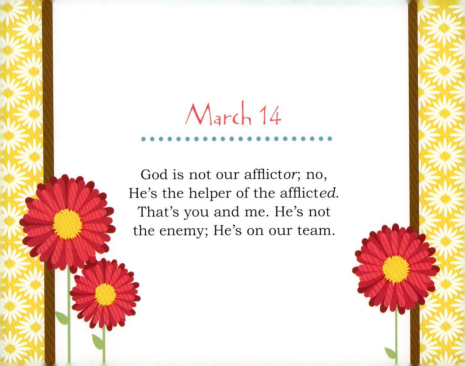

March 14

God is not our afflict*or*; no,
He's the helper of the afflict*ed*.
That's you and me. He's not
the enemy; He's on our team.

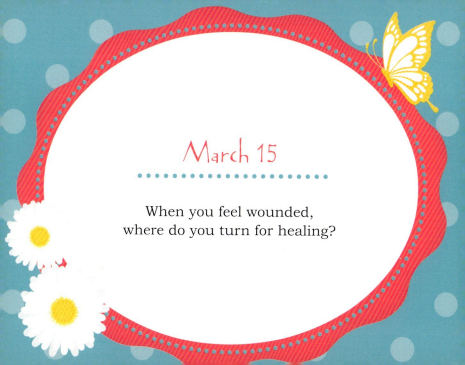

March 15

When you feel wounded,
where do you turn for healing?

March 16

Stress management professionals recommend that you engage in one weekly activity just for fun. But, hey, why stop at one?

March 17

*I will still be the same
when you are old and gray,
and I will take care of you.*

Isaiah 46:4 CEV

March 18

. . . .

Drag your thoughts away from your
troubles. . .by the ears, by the heels,
or any other way you can manage it.

MARK TWAIN

March 19

· ·

Jesus Himself stole away
for a rest break and encouraged
His buds to do likewise.

March 20

We are treasured. Cherished. Adored.
Papa God wants nothing more than
to cuddle with us, crooning His
comfort and peace into our
troubled hearts.
Anytime. Anywhere.

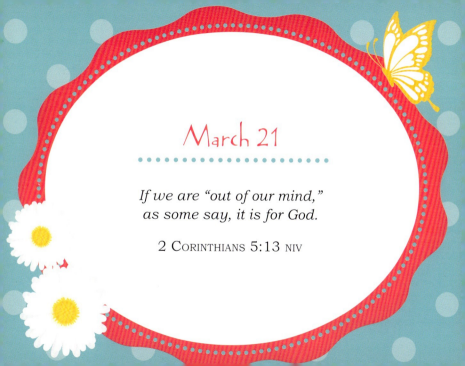

March 21

· ·

If we are "out of our mind,"
as some say, it is for God.

2 CORINTHIANS 5:13 NIV

March 22

We may not be able to eliminate stress from our crazy lives, but we *can* empower ourselves to weather the stress better by pursuing rejuvenating activities that refill our joy tanks rather than suck us bone dry.

March 23

. . . .

TIME TO LOL!

No woman is an island
(but she can dream!).

March 24

Mercy is completely undeserved;
that's what makes it so exquisitely
valuable. Take a moment and treasure
the free gift of God's mercy in giving
His Son as payment for your sins.

March 25

· ·

*When you have eaten and are
satisfied, praise the LORD your God
for the good land he has given you.*

DEUTERONOMY 8:10 NIV

March 26

· ·

Behave outwardly like Christ, pray for His
power, and your inner emotions and
thoughts will gradually transform
to become more Christlike.
Fake it at first if you have to—
the *act* becomes *fact* as God
changes you from
the outside in.

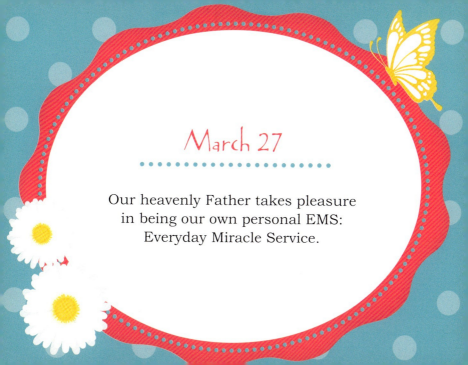

March 27

Our heavenly Father takes pleasure
in being our own personal EMS:
Everyday Miracle Service.

March 28

You don't love someone for their looks
or their clothes or for their fancy
car, but because they sing a
song only you can hear.

UNKNOWN

March 29

"First clean the inside of the cup and dish, and then the outside also will be clean."

MATTHEW 23:26 NIV

March 30

Like scum building up in the corners of the shower, emotional residue can dirty the edges of our peace without us even realizing it. As unsettling as it can be at the moment, it's important to deal with situations as they arise and not carry them around for weeks or even years like stinky loaded diapers.

March 31

Some say Christians should be sober
and serious and silent as the grave,
but I say Jesus came *out* of the grave,
and that's the best reason in
the world to celebrate!

April 1

There's absolutely nothing
you're tempted to worry about
that you won't be better off
talking to God about instead.

GREG LAURIE

April 2

....

Don't waste your time on
useless work, mere busywork,
the barren pursuits of darkness.

E͏PHESIANS 5:16 MSG

April 3

TIME TO LOL!

A socially acceptable way to
release frustration: organized sports.
(It's better than beating up your trash
can or shredding your panty hose.)

April 4

Girlfriends fill the holes in our
relationships with others,
especially the sinkholes.
Girlfriends make us laugh
when we least expect it.

April 5

Papa God didn't intend for our bodies to stay in the same position hour after hour or to perform the same function repeatedly without resting. Paced, daily time-outs for a few simple stretching exercises can bring immense relief to painful necks and tight shoulders.

April 6

· ·

Pride lands you flat on your face;
humility prepares you for honors.

PROVERBS 29:23 MSG

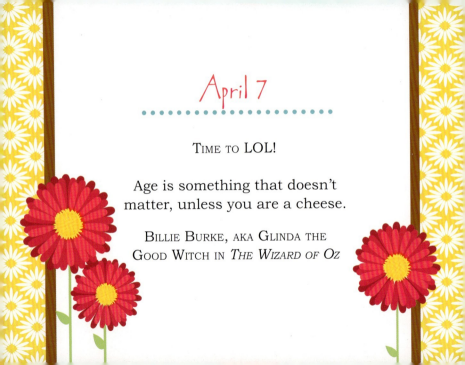

April 7

TIME TO LOL!

Age is something that doesn't matter, unless you are a cheese.

BILLIE BURKE, AKA GLINDA THE GOOD WITCH IN *THE WIZARD OF OZ*

April 8

Trust is the cornerstone to acquiring peace. We can relax in complete security knowing our Creator is looking out for our best interests. Relax. Uncoil. Chill. Let go of the steering wheel.

April 9

Marinating in faith produces
the choicest priority cuts.

April 10

· ·

When you lie down,
your sleep will be sweet.

PROVERBS 3:24 NIV

April 11

TIME TO LOL!

Life's made up of little
accomplishments—don't
obsess over the holes
and miss the doughnuts!

April 12

We must keep our arsenals full of ammo by memorizing verses and studying our Bibles so our flaming arrows are lit and ready to shoot the moment we're jumped by the enemy, the devil.

April 13

Today, read Isaiah 46:4 (NLT): *I will be your God throughout your lifetime—until your hair is white with age. I made you, and I will care for you. I will carry you along and save you.*

How does God's reassurance that He'll take care of you when you have snow on your roof affect the way you live today?

April 14

*I know everything you have done,
and you are not cold or hot.
I wish you were either one or the other.*

REVELATION 3:15 CEV

April 15

· ·

TIME TO LOL!

Set aside half an hour every day
to do all your worrying, then take
a nap during this period.

UNKNOWN

April 16

How do you replenish your
faith reserves on a daily basis?

April 17

We can't help the flat feet and connect-
the-dot freckles our children inherit,
but we *can* intentionally transfer
specific character-molding traits.
It's never too late to lay the foundation
for a strong and lasting faith dynasty!

April 18

* *

When my life was slipping away,
I remembered you—and in your
holy temple you heard my prayer.

JONAH 2:7 CEV

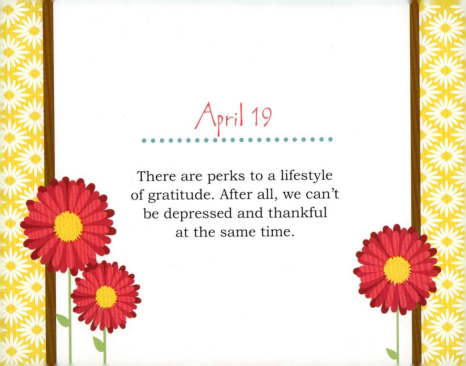

April 19

There are perks to a lifestyle
of gratitude. After all, we can't
be depressed and thankful
at the same time.

April 20

We go through turbulent seasons, but we have to remember that the storms won't last forever. Dawn always breaks after a long, dark night.

April 21

Pour out your feelings to Papa God.
He understands loss—His beloved
Son was ruthlessly beaten and killed.
Go ahead, pound on His chest. Scream.
Sob. He's a very *big* God. He can take it.

April 22

· ·

The righteous eat to their hearts'
content, but the stomach of the
wicked goes hungry.

PROVERBS 13:25 NIV

April 23

For fast-acting relief,
try slowing down.

LILY TOMLIN

April 24

God's specialty, His forte, His marvelous operational technique, is to use inadequate, frightened people to serve as His hands and feet. Yahweh's courage is more than enough.

April 25

Mother Teresa, a prayer warrior tiny in stature but enormous in spirit, once said, "God speaks in the silence of the heart. Listening is the beginning of prayer."

April 26

Happiness makes you smile;
sorrow can crush you.

PROVERBS 15:13 CEV

April 27

God is the Lord of details, you know.
And He loves to surprise us.

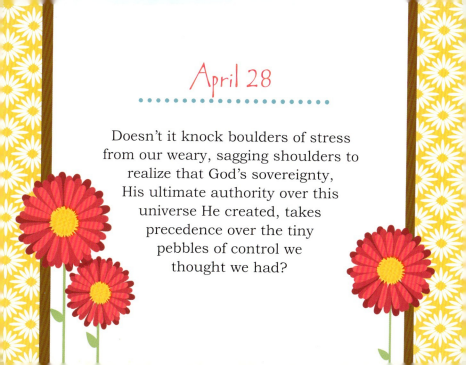

April 28

Doesn't it knock boulders of stress
from our weary, sagging shoulders to
realize that God's sovereignty,
His ultimate authority over this
universe He created, takes
precedence over the tiny
pebbles of control we
thought we had?

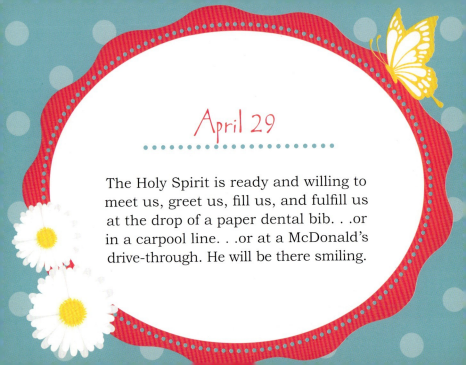

April 29

The Holy Spirit is ready and willing to meet us, greet us, fill us, and fulfill us at the drop of a paper dental bib. . .or in a carpool line. . .or at a McDonald's drive-through. He will be there smiling.

April 30

. . . .

I've decided that there's nothing better to do than go ahead and have a good time and get the most we can out of life.

ECCLESIASTES 3:12 MSG

May 1

Healing takes effort on our part; we can't just
sit like a limp, wounded lump and wait
for it to hit us. We have to dig deep
for the courage to reach out for
help from the very source of our
pain. Or so we perceive. But then
by God's grace we *will* find
what was really never lost.

May 2

· ·

Eternal life is the dessert
on the smorgasbord of faith.

May 3

All peace isn't created equal.
The world's peace is based on the
absence of conflict; God's peace
comes in the midst of conflict.

May 4

*A cord of three strands
is not quickly torn apart.*

ECCLESIASTES 4:12 NASB

May 5

· ·

Papa God's rejuvenating touch
of joy creates the ultimate face-lift!

May 6

Trust in our heavenly Father is meant to
literally become part of us. A lifestyle.
An underlying belief system that is
woven into the fabric of our being as
much as the color of our eyes.
Not something we have to remember
to apply. . .like sunscreen or lipstick.

May 7

We can either bless people or blast them with our tongues—like little lethal cannons. I choose to be a blesser. How about you?

May 8

He gives a greater grace. . . .
"God is opposed to the proud,
but gives grace to the humble."

JAMES 4:6 NASB

May 9

TIME TO LOL!

I used to pride myself on quick, logical decisions: the green shoes or the teal? Now I stare slack-jawed at the shoe store and go home with six different colors. Spouse thinks I'm indecisive, but I'm just not sure.

May 10

Faith is taking the first step even
when we don't see the
whole staircase.

MARTIN LUTHER KING JR.

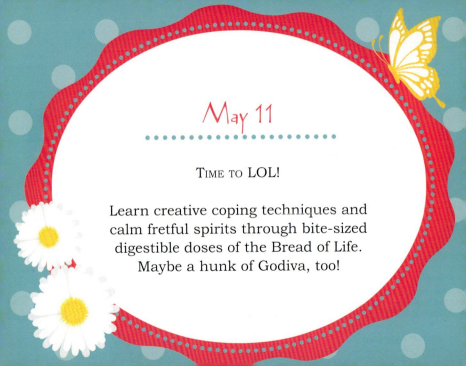

May 11

TIME TO LOL!

Learn creative coping techniques and calm fretful spirits through bite-sized digestible doses of the Bread of Life. Maybe a hunk of Godiva, too!

May 12

· ·

If we only do as much as we can do,
then the Lord will take over and
do what only He can do.

May 13

· ·

A cheerful heart is good medicine,
but a crushed spirit dries up the bones.
PROVERBS 17:22 NIV

What does Proverbs 17:22
tell us about the importance
of having fun?

May 14

Today, kick seriousness out for the evening
and plan a night of hysteria. Include the
people and things (foods, games, movies,
goofy clothes) that make you smile,
and indulge in a little hilarity.
Your stress level will drop five floors!

May 15

TIME TO LOL!

Knowing about God and knowing God
is the same difference between reading
a cordon bleu recipe and being Julia Child.

May 16

Love is kind and patient, never jealous, boastful, proud, or rude. Love isn't selfish or quick tempered. It doesn't keep a record of wrongs that others do. Love rejoices in the truth, but not in evil.

1 CORINTHIANS 13:4–6 CEV

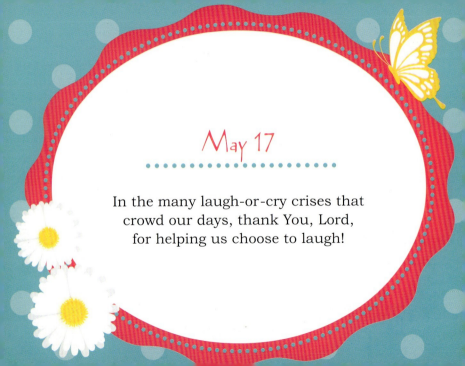

May 17

In the many laugh-or-cry crises that
crowd our days, thank You, Lord,
for helping us choose to laugh!

May 18

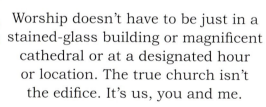

Worship doesn't have to be just in a
stained-glass building or magnificent
cathedral or at a designated hour
or location. The true church isn't
the edifice. It's us, you and me.

May 19

Have you ever been so moved that you burst forth in spontaneous worship? If not, you should try it sometime. There's nothing so exhilarating!

May 20

. . . .

Don't hit back;
discover beauty in everyone.

ROMANS 12:17 MSG

May 21

· ·

You are *not* Superwoman with nerves of
steel. Or guts either. Stress is kryptonite,
and it's out to rip off your cape and
reduce you to a pile of quivering,
ineffective mush. Okay, that's the
bad news. How about some good?
When stress gets the best of us,
the heavenly Father is there
to put us back together again.

May 22

Add yourself to your daily
to-do list. You're important!

May 23

TIME TO LOL!

Side effects of a late-afternoon nap can include an interesting maze of facial furrows from the pile of unfolded laundry upon which your head lands.

May 24

· ·

We will tell the next generation
the praiseworthy deeds of the LORD,
his power, and the wonders he has done.

PSALM 78:4 NIV

May 25

TIME TO LOL!

God's divinely orchestrated levity
of love plays out all around us
through His marvelous creation:
take, for example, aardvarks,
spoonbill platypuses,
and cowlicks.

May 26

. . . .

TIME TO LOL!

Repetitive redundancy. No, this is not the name of a new rock group. It's what you should do to take your frantic self down a notch: crochet, do needlepoint, play piano scales. . . . You need a calm, repetitive, manual task that takes minimal brain power. Chopping firewood doesn't count.

May 27

We should learn from our mistakes, sure, but then shed the guilt like a moth-eaten winter coat. Don a fresh spring outfit, and look ahead. Our past prepares us for the future if we're open to the present.

May 28

· ·

*I will sing for joy at
the works of Your hands.*

PSALM 92:4 NASB

May 29

Take a moment and praise our Lord and
Savior for His all-powerful sovereignty.
Remember, He's large and in charge!

May 30

Negativity is habit forming. Channeling Eeyore becomes the soundtrack for our subconscious thoughts. Those mopey, self-deprecating donkey thoughts wear us down and wear us out before we even realize the source of the erosion. Why settle for defeat when, with a few minor attitude adjustments, we could open the door for *amazing* possibilities?

May 31

TIME TO LOL!

In my humble but accurate opinion,
naps are an essential pause in
the nonstop stress of our day.
When I miss my nappy,
ain't nobody happy.

June 1

. . . .

*A man's counsel is
sweet to his friend.*

PROVERBS 27:9 NASB

June 2

Shake the mental Etch A Sketch.
Get out the attitude chain saw.
Replace negative thoughts
with a positive spin.

June 3

Tack on hope. Add the magical three-
letter word *yet*. When tacked on
at the end of a negative thought,
it miraculously transforms
"I can't" perspectives into
"I can, with a little more time."

June 4

Think a moment of the top three negative messages you routinely send yourself. Now practice tweaking your tone, speaking like your own BFF, and tacking on hope. Take the bold step from negative to positive thinking!

June 5

· ·

Love wisdom like a sister.

PROVERBS 7:4 NLT

June 6

· ·

Love has nothing to do with what
you are expecting to get—only with
what you are expecting to
give—which is everything.

KATHARINE HEPBURN

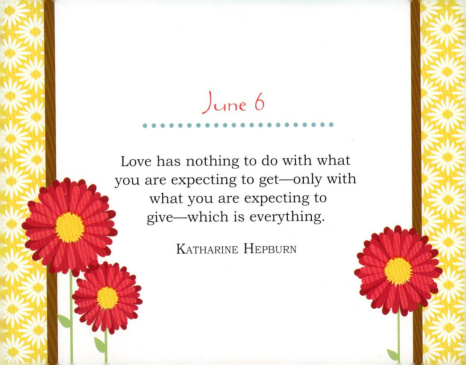

June 7

TIME TO LOL!

Opportunity knocks softly,
but temptation parks its fat derriere
on the doorbell, scarfing chocolate.

June 8

Walk, run, ski, work out, join roller derby—whatever waxes your eyebrows—but make exercise a priority. Do it for *you*.

June 9

· ·

The troubles of my heart are enlarged;
bring me out of my distresses.

PSALM 25:17 NASB

June 10

Concern draws us to God.
Worry pulls us from him.

JOANNA WEAVER

June 11

God doesn't want us to be washed-out dishrags. God is *not* glorified when we are so exhausted that we don't realize we're brushing our hair with a toothbrush or trying to pay for groceries with our library card. Scale down, pull back, and simplify.

June 12

Read the instructions! Make a plan—and stick to it—to read and study God's Word daily. This is how we replenish our depleted reserves.

June 13

Then, because you belong to Christ Jesus, God will bless you with peace that no one can completely understand. And this peace will control the way you think and feel.

PHILIPPIANS 4:7 CEV

June 14

As adults, we don't often have the luxury of free hours, but we can carve free minutes out of each day if we diligently simplify and unclog those constipated calendars. That, dear sister, is when we reconnect with that summer morning feeling.

June 15

. . . .

Lord, help me remember that the worst
thing that could possibly happen to
me today is that I'd wake up
in heaven in Your arms.
That's exciting!

June 16

Over the years I have honed the art of worry into a science. I've systematically and diligently transformed molehills into mountains. I've whipped pesky irritants into frothy, acetic colon-coaters and fretted over annoying burdens until they invaded my dreams.

June 17

* *

Weeping may stay for the night,
but rejoicing comes in the morning.

PSALM 30:5 NIV

June 18

The Lord doesn't ask us
to understand; He only
asks us to trust.

June 19

. . . .

Laughter is our lifeline when we're
sinking into the pit of rigidity, when
we're so absorbed in the stressful details
of our lives that we're missing the fun.

June 20

TIME TO LOL!

I heard on the radio that scientists
have discovered a natural extract
in chocolate that cleans teeth better
than toothpaste. Hey, I'll bite!

June 21

Love never gives up, never loses faith,
is always hopeful, and endures
through every circumstance.

1 Corinthians 13:7 nlt

June 22

Jesus came to earth as the
Creator in created form.
He loves us *that* much!

June 23

To change my behavior, I first have to change my way of thinking. The way I act starts with what's happening in my head. No stinkin' thinkin' for me!

June 24

Are you overextending yourself? Spreading your time or energies too thin? Regardless of how well intentioned we are, we're only human, and the Master Designer, who created us and *knows* our limitations, wants us to set parameters to pick and choose the way we expend our finite energies.

June 25

For God has not given us a spirit of
fear and timidity, but of power,
love, and self-discipline.

2 TIMOTHY 1:7 NLT

June 26

Make daily time with Papa God a priority. Tight schedules are no excuse.

June 27

Consistently refresh your reserves—
your level of dependency on God's
grace and patience is reflected in
your grace and patience
toward others.

June 28

. . . .

TIME TO LOL!

Bette Davis was right:
"Old age ain't no place for sissies."

June 29

*"Call on me and come and pray to me,
and I will listen to you."*

JEREMIAH 29:12 NIV

June 30

. . . .

God is in the miracle business, and He
"*is* able to do far more abundantly
beyond all that we ask or think,
according to the power that works
within us" (Ephesians 3:20 NASB,
emphasis added). That power,
of course, is His enormous,
undefeatable power.

July 1

TIME TO LOL!

A wonderful definition of feminine might:
True strength is breaking a chocolate
bar into four pieces bare-handed—
and then eating only one.

July 2

· ·

I know God will not give me
anyting I can't handle. I just wish
He didn't trust me so much.

MOTHER TERESA

July 3

Pray without ceasing.

1 Thessalonians 5:17 NASB

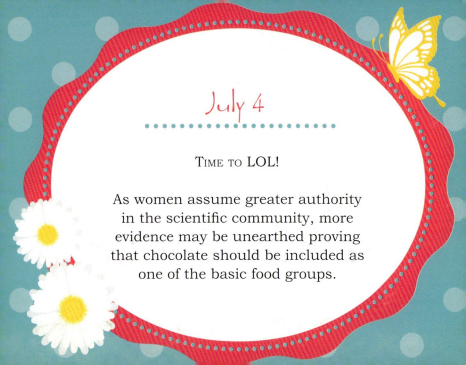

July 4

TIME TO LOL!

As women assume greater authority in the scientific community, more evidence may be unearthed proving that chocolate should be included as one of the basic food groups.

July 5

What's the answer for us matrons of muddle? We must lower our expectations. That's right, pitch perfectionism, lose the legalism, cast off comparisons. Limbo under that self-imposed bar of spotlessness!

July 6

God wants us to invest our precious minutes on earth in people, not things. Focus on pursuing those whose souls hang in the balance of eternity.

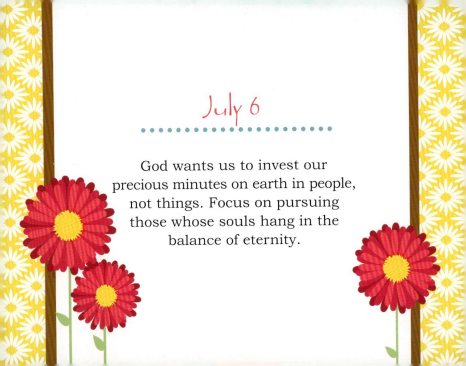

July 7

. . . .

We can make our plans,
but the Lord determines our steps.

Proverbs 16:9 NLT

July 8

· ·

Faith can move mountains,
but don't be surprised if
God hands you a shovel.

UNKNOWN

July 9

Pride is an underhanded thief. It sneaks
up and robs us of the heart-changing
gratitude that is a by-product of
knowing—and acknowledging—
that our attributes, abilities,
and accolades are simply gifts
for our Creator. Gifts wrapped
in love and tied with
a bow of grace.

July 10

When you get to the
end of your rope, you'll find
Papa God waiting with a ladder.

July 11

· ·

*Nothing in all creation is
hidden from God's sight.*

HEBREWS 4:13 NIV

July 12

Why does God care about stubborn, rebellious creatures? Why should He waste His time rescuing hapless victims of their own bad choices? We certainly don't deserve His mercy. Yet He lovingly extends it to us anyway. Over and over and over again.

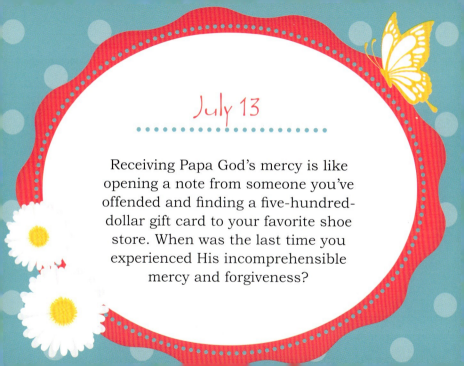

July 13

Receiving Papa God's mercy is like opening a note from someone you've offended and finding a five-hundred-dollar gift card to your favorite shoe store. When was the last time you experienced His incomprehensible mercy and forgiveness?

July 14

TIME TO LOL!

A big ole hunk of peanut butter fudge is the best way to gag that obnoxious skinny inner gal trying to bust through the waist rolls.

July 15

. . . .

"If you had faith even as small as a mustard seed, you could say to this mountain, 'Move from here to there,' and it would move. Nothing would be impossible."

MATTHEW 17:20 NLT

July 16

Colossians 2:7 advises us, "Let your lives be built on him. . .and you will overflow with thankfulness" (NLT). What steps can you take to make living thankfully an everyday habit?

July 17

· ·

In the midst of my rushed life, Lord,
give me patience to wait on You
to act in Your own perfect timing.

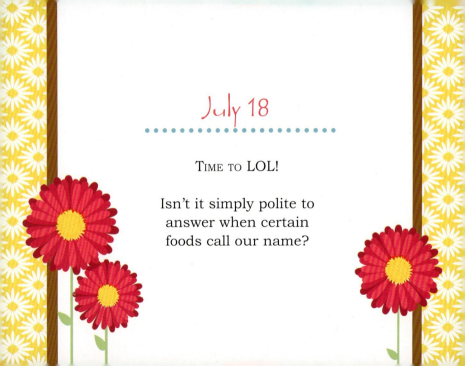

July 18

TIME TO LOL!

Isn't it simply polite to
answer when certain
foods call our name?

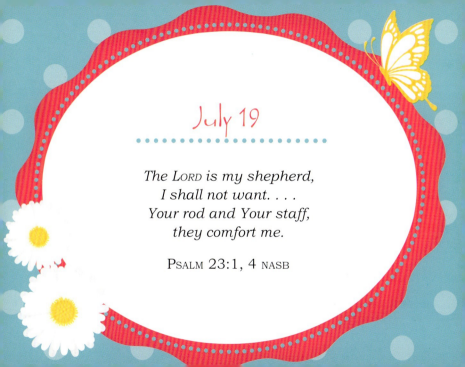

July 19

· ·

The Lord is my shepherd,
I shall not want. . . .
Your rod and Your staff,
they comfort me.

PSALM 23:1, 4 NASB

July 20

Living water:
Why settle for a trickle when
God wants to give you Niagara Falls?

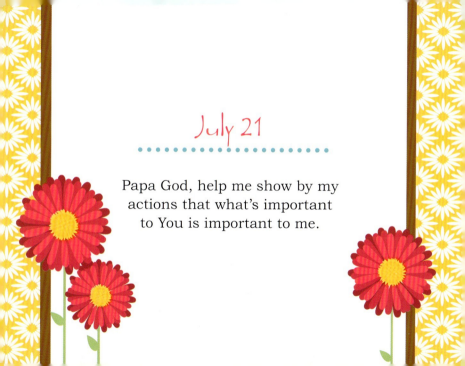

July 21

Papa God, help me show by my
actions that what's important
to You is important to me.

July 22

. . . .

Joy and laughter are soul sisters;
they travel together.

July 23

· ·

You, LORD, are. . .
the One who lifts my head high.

PSALM 3:3 NIV

July 24

Time to **LOL!**

Sometimes I wish I'd grabbed
the glue stick instead
of my lipstick.

July 25

TIME TO **LOL**!

It must've been a woman who
coined the phrase "wee hours"
on a midnight potty run.

July 26

The more I've watched the connection
between humor and creativity,
the more I've realized there is
very little difference between the
terms, "Aha!" and "Ha Ha!"

VATCHE BARTEKIAN,
STRESS MANAGEMENT SPECIALIST

July 27

· ·

Be anxious for nothing, but in everything by prayer and supplication with thanksgiving let your requests be made known to God. And the peace of God, which surpasses all comprehension, will guard your hearts and your minds in Christ Jesus.

PHILIPPIANS 4:6–7 NASB

July 28

TIME TO LOL!

I suffer from CDD: Chocolate Deficit
Disorder. A choco-infusion every two
hours is necessary for temperament
stability and the mental health
of those around me.

July 29

Our Lord specializes in repairing rips in relationships. He's more than happy to provide the cord strength when two of the strands become frayed.

July 30

You don't have to like someone to pray for
them. But you may be surprised
how bitterness evolves into
something quite different
when you're on your knees.

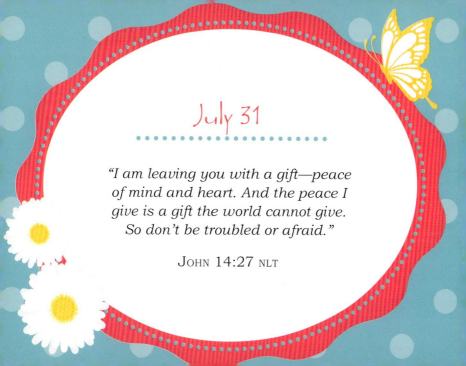

July 31

"I am leaving you with a gift—peace of mind and heart. And the peace I give is a gift the world cannot give. So don't be troubled or afraid."

JOHN 14:27 NLT

August 1

Wonder is involuntary praise.

EDWARD YOUNG

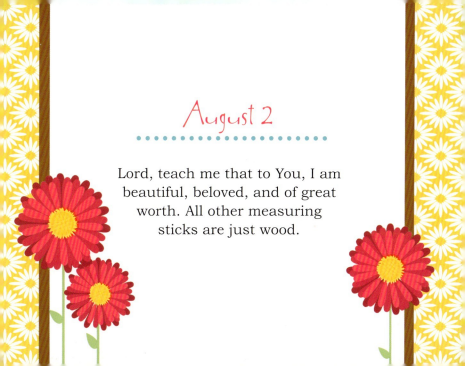

August 2

Lord, teach me that to You, I am beautiful, beloved, and of great worth. All other measuring sticks are just wood.

August 3

Our heavenly Father doesn't
care how much we know, but He
wants to know how much we care.

August 4

And God will wipe the
tears from every face.

Isaiah 25:8 msg

August 5

T<small>IME TO</small> LOL!

Let she who is guiltless cast the first stone.
Who hasn't stashed Tootsie Rolls among
the potted plants or hidden M&M'S
in her ibuprofen bottle? Or buried
telltale Snickers wrappers inside
balled-up paper towels
in the trash can?

August 6

TIME TO LOL!

There must be a way to use
gravity to our advantage.
Maybe ditching our bras would
pull the wrinkles out of our faces.

August 7

Lord, help me live my life out loud,
like the melodic crescendo of a
beautiful orchestra. Not a foghorn.

August 8

"Be sure of this: I am with you always, even to the end of the age."

MATTHEW 28:20 NLT

August 9

Boogie. Belly dance. Polka. Get your
bad self down. Music has the magical ability
to speed us up, calm us down, distract
(in a good way) and inspire us—tap into
this simple source of happiness
(pun intended)!

August 10

Sometimes prayer is all it takes
to transform loathing into loving.

August 11

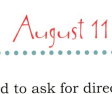

It's so hard to ask for directions when we get lost. But Papa God is standing there beside the road holding the map; we just have to stop and roll down the window.

August 12

*I sought the L*ORD*, and He answered me,*
and delivered me from all my fears.

PSALM 34:4 NASB

August 13

It's tempting to pray for the elimination
of obstacles in our lives, but the creek
would never dance if Papa God
removed the rocks.

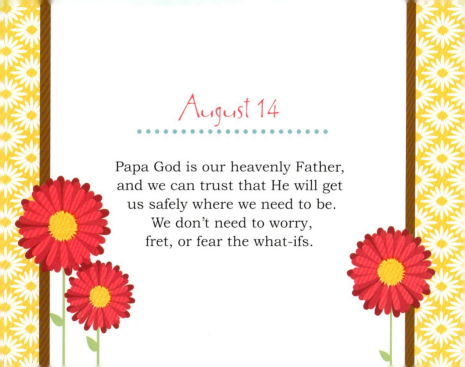

August 14

Papa God is our heavenly Father,
and we can trust that He will get
us safely where we need to be.
We don't need to worry,
fret, or fear the what-ifs.

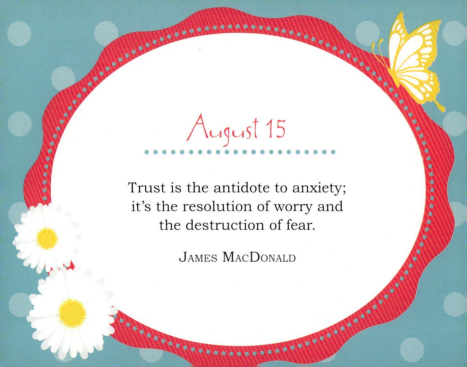

August 15

Trust is the antidote to anxiety;
it's the resolution of worry and
the destruction of fear.

JAMES MACDONALD

August 16

• •

Come near to God and
he will come near to you.

JAMES 4:8 NIV

August 17

Remember, the almighty
creator of the universe set the
precedent by resting after
a strenuous workweek.

August 18

TIME TO LOL!

Our personalities are reflected in our snacks of choice. Maybe instead of the traditional four personality types (choleric, sanguine, melancholic, and phlegmatic), we should switch to tortilla chip, pretzel, cheese curl, or potato chip. Women would certainly understand the implications better.

August 19

Infinite possibilities. . .
are born of faith.

MOTHER TERESA

August 20

Wait patiently for the LORD.
Be brave and courageous.

PSALM 27:14 NLT

August 21

Do you know the one stress reliever that women need every day but often neglect? Nope, it's not love, sex, or chocolate engorgement. Are you ready? It's *fun*! That's right—good ole giggle-producing, endorphin-generating, tension-popping fun!

August 22

Why don't we dance more?
Even the dignified prophetess Miriam
grabbed her tambourine and cut
loose with her girlfriends. I, too,
want to hear God's music and
do His celebration dance.

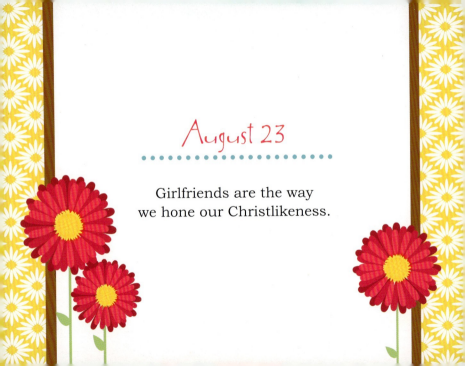

August 23

· ·

Girlfriends are the way
we hone our Christlikeness.

August 24

*In peace I will both
lie down and sleep.*

PSALM 4:8 NASB

August 25

Time to LOL!

These earth suits are only temporary.
Heaven will not have beauty pageants.
And I really don't think it would
be heaven without Oreos.

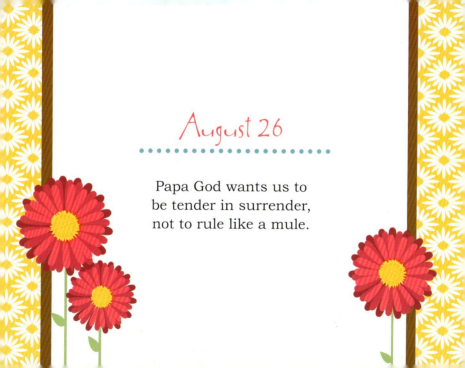

August 26

Papa God wants us to
be tender in surrender,
not to rule like a mule.

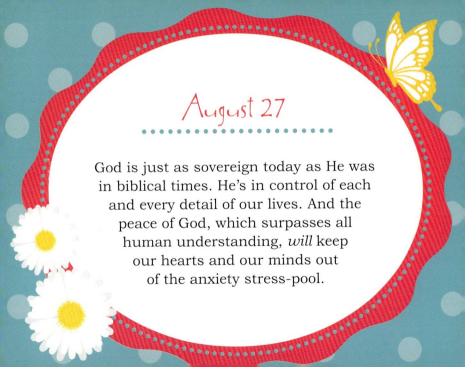

August 27

God is just as sovereign today as He was in biblical times. He's in control of each and every detail of our lives. And the peace of God, which surpasses all human understanding, *will* keep our hearts and our minds out of the anxiety stress-pool.

August 28

*We know that God is always at work
for the good of everyone who loves him.*

ROMANS 8:28 CEV

August 29

Prayers are verbal faith.

August 30

TIME TO LOL!

Ulcer is *kids* spelled backward.
Well, it should be anyway.

August 31

My best stress reliever has been to remind myself in the midst of the fray that the most important things in my world are my people. *My* peeps. Those beautiful souls God has entrusted to my care for a few short years.

September 1

. . . .

Rest in the Lord and
wait patiently for Him.

PSALM 37:7 NASB

September 2

TIME TO LOL!

The way I see it, I'm actually being thoughtful by ignoring my mop and dust rag. I'm eliminating the sinful temptation for friends who might fall short in comparison.

September 3

When I'm plugged into Your power source, Lord, it's amazing how long I can march while beating my big drum!

September 4

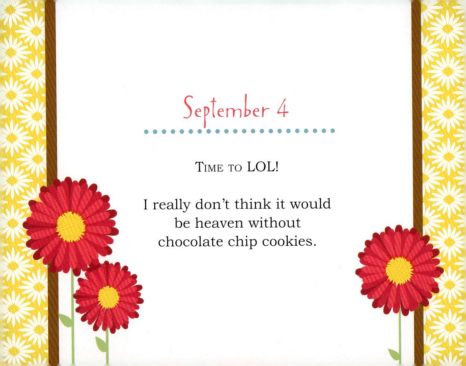

TIME TO LOL!

I really don't think it would
be heaven without
chocolate chip cookies.

September 5

My flesh and my heart may fail,
but God is the strength of my
heart and my portion forever.

PSALM 73:26 NASB

September 6

I've come to realize Jesus was absolutely right in Luke 12:25–26 (big *duh*—isn't He always right?): "Has anyone by fussing before the mirror ever gotten taller by so much as an inch? If fussing can't even do that, why fuss at all?" (MSG). I mean really, what's all the fuss about?

September 7

Generosity is faith with legs.

September 8

Caving to the dark side doesn't *have* to be our destiny, Luke! We have the Force above all other forces, the one true, living God, willing and able to provide armor (for defense) and ammo (for offense) in our ongoing battle against temptation.

September 9

Resist the devil and he will flee from you.

JAMES 4:7 NASB

September 10

God's love for us isn't dependent on anything we do or don't do, blab or omit. Our Father's love itself—not anything we can contrive, create, or earn—is what makes us whole and holy.

September 11

In what specific ways does Papa God's
unconditional love make you feel
cuddled, cherished, peaceful?

September 12

An ounce of mother is
worth a pound of clergy.

SPANISH PROVERB

September 13

*"No eye has seen, no ear has heard,
and no mind has imagined what
God has prepared for
those who love him."*

1 CORINTHIANS 2:9 NLT

September 14

Certain thoughts are prayers.
There are moments when,
whatever be the attitude of the
body, the soul is on its knees.

Victor Hugo, *Les Misérables*

September 15

I don't want to approach prayer as a chore. I'm not reporting for duty or giving God instructions on what's best for me. Nor do I want my prayer life to consist merely of rhino-in-the-road desperation pleas to NeedGodNOW.com. I come with a humble heart, an open mind, and a thirsty spirit. I *cherish* spending time with Him.

September 16

Is prayer more of a single event or a
continuous mind-set for you? Prayer can
become our last resort rather than
our first resort if we don't regard
communication with Christ
as important as breathing.
Even before our prayers are
answered, we benefit from
the immense blessing
of His loving company.

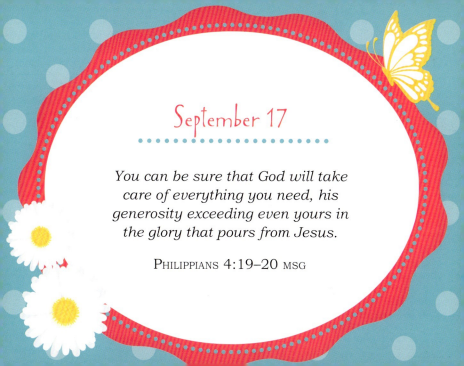

September 17

*You can be sure that God will take
care of everything you need, his
generosity exceeding even yours in
the glory that pours from Jesus.*

PHILIPPIANS 4:19–20 MSG

September 18

It's a crying shame to devote our lives
to the goal of standing at the door
to eternity with gorgeous size
4 bodies, tanned to perfection,
foreheads silky smooth, eyes bag-free,
hair gleaming, arms Dumbo flapless,
thighs tapioca-free. What good is it?
God will not be impressed. He'll be
looking at our insides, at our hearts.

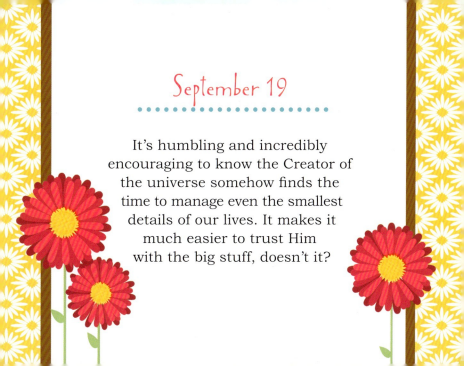

September 19

It's humbling and incredibly
encouraging to know the Creator of
the universe somehow finds the
time to manage even the smallest
details of our lives. It makes it
much easier to trust Him
with the big stuff, doesn't it?

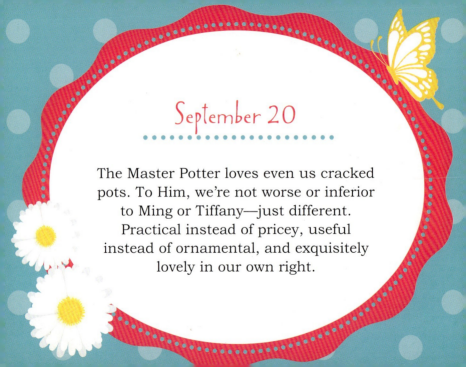

September 20

The Master Potter loves even us cracked pots. To Him, we're not worse or inferior to Ming or Tiffany—just different. Practical instead of pricey, useful instead of ornamental, and exquisitely lovely in our own right.

September 21

Life is made up of little
accomplishments; these are what
we should make a *big* deal about.

September 22

Master of the universe who calmed the
stormy seas, send me a chill pill
when problems seem unfixable.
Remind me that everyday
miracles are Your thing.
It's what You do.

September 23

TIME TO LOL!

One of the most important and long-lasting relationships we cultivate is with these earth suits God has entrusted to us for a limited time. Depending on the condition in which we maintain them, our bodies can be comforting, a source of pleasure, a vehicle for adventure, or a restrictive straitjacket.

September 24

Let's admit it—none of us wants our
temple to fall into ruins. With a sturdy
foundation of prevention and a slap
or two of maintenance mortar,
our flesh-and-blood cathedrals can glorify
God for decades to come without one
brick crumbling from neglect.

September 25

We are the temple
of the living God.

2 CORINTHIANS 6:16 NIV

September 26

Has your focus been on decorating your earth suit? What steps can you take to shift emphasis to the inside rather than the outside?

September 27

God can make anyone into anything.
He made ninety-year-old Sarah a mother,
and Rahab, a prostitute, an honored
ancestor of Jesus. He morphed a lonely
little Jewish orphan into gorgeous Queen
Esther. And He's not finished with me yet!

September 28

When I start to worry or obsess,
I recite the facts I know to be true:
God is in control; He loves me;
He wants what's best for me,
even though my ideas may
not be His; I only find peace
by resting in His will.

September 29

*God, the source of hope, will fill you
completely with joy and peace because
you trust in him. Then you will overflow
with confident hope through the
power of the Holy Spirit.*

ROMANS 15:13 NLT

September 30

Papa God never meant for us to keep going 900 mph all day. He built triggers into our bodies to cue us when it's time to escape consciousness. Wise people, such as notable nappers Albert Einstein, Thomas Edison, Winston Churchill, John F. Kennedy, and Ronald Reagan, listen to those cues.

October 1

· ·

Jesus said, "Let's go off by ourselves to a quiet place and rest awhile." He said this because there were so many people coming and going that Jesus and his apostles didn't even have time to eat. So they left by boat for a quiet place, where they could be alone.
Mark 6:31–32 nlt

Why do you think stealing away for rest was so important to Jesus? Why should it be important to you?

October 2

. . . .

My determination is to transfer this
habit of worry into an instant moment
of prayer and leaving it with God.

CHARLES SWINDOLL

October 3

···

How blessed is the
man who trusts in You!

PSALM 84:12 NASB

October 4

The nice thing about the future is
that it always starts tomorrow.

UNKNOWN

October 5

The Bible says our bodies are God's temples. If we, as temple caretakers, are to withstand battering gales and the onslaught of relentless enemy attacks, we must fortify our living structures from within!

October 6

There are no coincidences in the *grace notes* of our lives. Grace notes—the little daily special touches from Papa God that let us know He has our backs— are the everyday miracles that reflect God's sovereignty, His supreme power and authority over every detail of our lives.

October 7

We know how much God loves us,
and we have put our trust in his love.

1 JOHN 4:16 NLT

October 8

When we turn control of our lives over to our Lord, everlasting life is ours. Not just the promise of heaven when we die but the glorious opportunity to live our lives walking beside our Abba Father, our Papa God, *today.*

October 9

Developing patience is like an oyster creating a rare pearl—we shouldn't pray for it unless we're prepared to withstand the long, grit-grinding process that produces it.

October 10

What-ifs often steal our peace and add to our
emotional turmoil. We must remind
ourselves that the what-ifs aren't real.
That's Satan sticking his dirty,
rotten fingers into our hearts
and minds to steal the peace
Papa God promises if
we depend on Him.

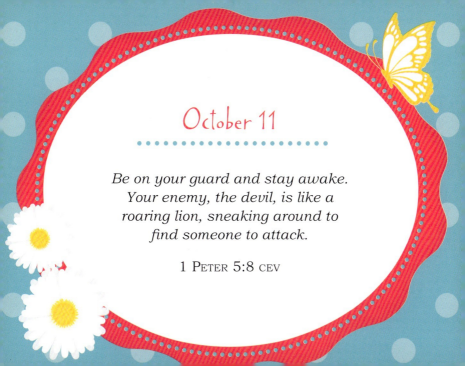

October 11

*Be on your guard and stay awake.
Your enemy, the devil, is like a
roaring lion, sneaking around to
find someone to attack.*

1 Peter 5:8 cev

October 12

Jesus is not just our Messiah,
Prince of Peace, and Savior.
He is our role model as a human
facing real, heart-slamming
adversity, our "God in a bod."

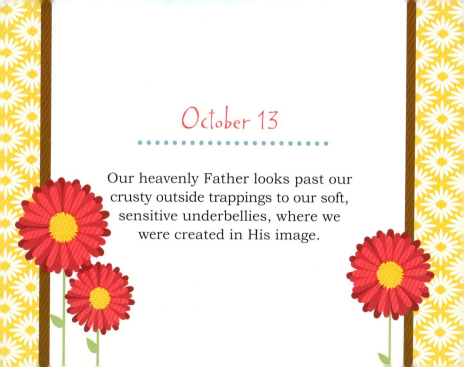

October 13

Our heavenly Father looks past our crusty outside trappings to our soft, sensitive underbellies, where we were created in His image.

October 14

P: Placing
E: Each
A: Aggravation at
C: Christ's feet. . .
E: Expectantly!

October 15

· ·

Why, my soul, are you downcast?. . .
Put your hope in God, for I will
yet praise him.

PSALM 42:11 NIV

October 16

If, for whatever reason, we can't remove
a temptation, we must remove
ourselves from the temptation.
Get thee out of there, girl!
Don't stand nekked in front
of a speeding freight train!

October 17

God measures our success
by faithfulness, not results.
Aren't you glad He cares more
about the ingredients than
whether the soufflé flopped?

October 18

Our Creator is standing by with a life preserver as we tread water in the stress-pool of everyday life. That buoyant ring meant to hold our heads above water is our Father's inexplicable infilling peace.

October 19

"*My peace I give you. I do not give to you as the world gives. Do not let your hearts be troubled and do not be afraid.*"

JOHN 14:27 NIV

October 20

You gain strength, courage, and
confidence by every experience in
which you really stop to look fear
in the face. You must do the thing
which you think you cannot do.

ELEANOR ROOSEVELT

October 21

· ·

TIME TO LOL!

Containing joy is like trying
to repress the freckle gene.

October 22

. . . .

If God used Balaam's donkey and
Peter's rooster to do His work,
He can use me, too!

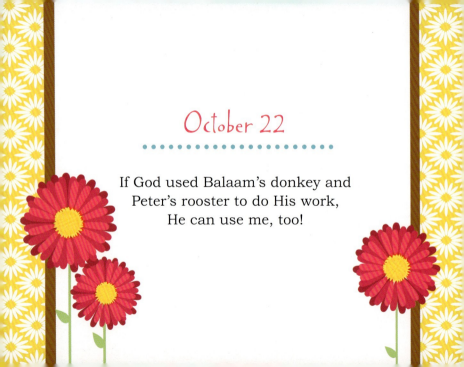

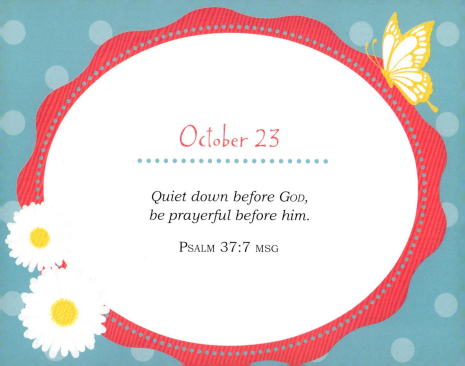

October 23

Quiet down before GOD,
be prayerful before him.

PSALM 37:7 MSG

October 24

· ·

Sometimes failure is Papa God's
way of saying, "Wait, My child. . .
this just isn't the right time."

October 25

What good are spiritual gifts
if we stuff them in our closets
or underneath our beds and
never open them?

October 26

Have you ever lost something then found it right in front of you? Life is like that. We search for answers and get uptight and stressed out, when the source of knowledge is in our possession the whole time. It's called the Bible.

October 27

So let's not get tired of doing what is good. At just the right time we will reap a harvest of blessing if we don't give up.

GALATIANS 6:9 NLT

October 28

The things I've found that once
were lost become oh, so much
more precious. Like faith.
And German chocolate. Mmm.

October 29

. . . .

I worship the Creator of butterflies,
humpback whales, three-toed sloths,
puppies, rainbows, waterfalls, and
sunbeams. How can I *not* smile?

October 30

. . . .

God had us—you and me—in
mind to be the focus of His love even
before the creation of the world.
What a calming, reassuring thought!

October 31

· ·

Long before he laid down earth's foundations,
he had us in mind, had settled on us
as the focus of his love, to be made
whole and holy by his love.

EPHESIANS 1:4 MSG

November 1

TIME TO LOL!

No diet will remove all the fat
from your body because the brain
is entirely fat. Without a brain,
you might look good, but all you
could do is run for public office.

GEORGE BERNARD SHAW

November 2

Life isn't always fair,
but God is always God.

November 3

Never forget that the best stress
reliever we have is each other!

November 4

....

He will cover you with his feathers,
and under his wings you will find refuge.

PSALM 91:4 NIV

November 5

Peace, in the midst of life's chaos.
Peace, that jumping-off platform for
inexplicable joy. Peace, that illusive,
anxiety-free place of freedom we
long for. Only when our trust is
anchored in God can we find peace.

November 6

Even sawed-off stumps will eventually become majestic, towering evergreens if they just keep sending out sprouts.

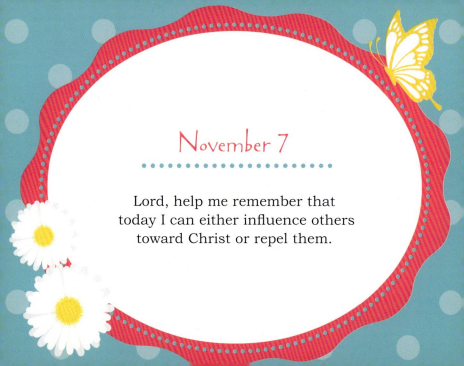

November 7

Lord, help me remember that today I can either influence others toward Christ or repel them.

November 8

We must get rid of everything that slows us down, especially the sin that just won't let go. And we must be determined to run the race that is ahead of us.

Hebrews 12:1 CEV

November 9

Our BFF is there for us through svelte
and bloated, sweet and grumpy,
thoughtful and insensitive.
How much more can we count
on our Blessed Friend
Forever—Papa God—
to be there for us?

November 10

A hope-filled person will realize that
abundant life in Christ isn't about
simply enduring the storm but also
about learning to dance in the puddles.
Let's grab our galoshes and boogie!

November 11

Remember how to laugh. A real,
honest-to-goodness, gurgling-from-the-guts
laugh. The kind that acts as a catalyst
to release the joy of the Lord in your
soul and color your future with
hope for a better tomorrow.

November 12

························

You will keep in perfect peace all
who trust in you, all whose
thoughts are fixed on you!

Isaiah 26:3 nlt

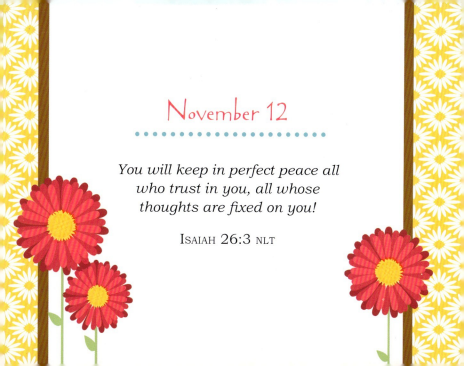

November 13

. . . .

Never give up! David picked
up five stones, not just one,
when he went out to face Goliath!

November 14

· ·

You can straighten your posture and adjust your face, but if the change doesn't come from the inside out, it won't stick. God is our Interior Decorator. Only He can provide that inner joy that projects outward and lifts our heads.

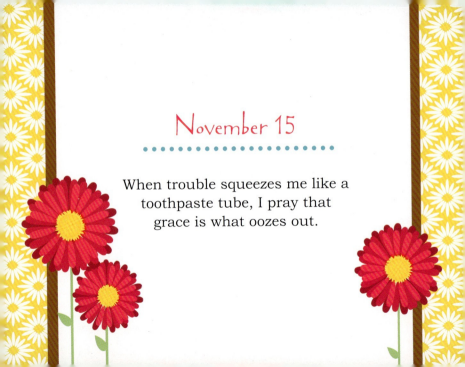

November 15

When trouble squeezes me like a
toothpaste tube, I pray that
grace is what oozes out.

November 16

*"For the L*ord *your God is living among you. He is a mighty savior. He will take delight in you with gladness. With his love, he will calm all your fears. He will rejoice over you with joyful songs."*

Zephaniah 3:17 nlt

November 17

God is in the business of using tiny slivers of what's left over to do mighty things. He accomplishes amazing miracles with remnants!

November 18

Prayer is not just spiritual
punctuation; it's every
word of our life's story.

November 19

Prayer is the least and
the most we can do.

November 20

· · · · · · · · · · · · · · · · · ·

Laugh with your happy friends
when they're happy; share tears
when they're down.

Romans 12:15 MSG

November 21

TIME TO LOL!

Weight control is no piece of
cake. You know it's true:
sugar shows and money talks,
but chocolate sings!

November 22

God's specialty is making positives
from negatives. In His garden of life,
cow-patty fertilizer produces
glorious flower blossoms.

November 23

. . . .

Can you think of five things to
be grateful for this very minute?

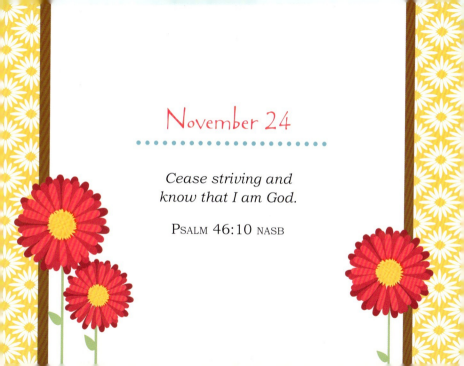

November 24

* *

*Cease striving and
know that I am God.*

Psalm 46:10 NASB

November 25

. . . .

It is not enough for a man to
pray cream and live skim milk.

HENRY WARD BEECHER

November 26

· ·

Laughter reflects a joyful heart!
Who doesn't like to hang out with
joyful, uplifting people?

November 27

I choose to love others for who
they are, not for what they do or
don't do. Lord, help me to remember
that the next time I encounter
my overflowing trash can.

November 28

Trust in the LORD with all your heart;
do not depend on your own understanding.
Seek his will in all you do, and he will
show you which path to take.

PROVERBS 3:5–6 NLT

November 29

Trust: such an intimate form of faith.
Trust should cling to us like a second
skin. Thankfully, Papa God knows
that it's a learning process for all of us.
He's patiently waiting for our level of
reliance to catch up and override our
not-so-common sense as we take
the plunge into trust.

November 30

Don't be a wimp! Be a warrior!
Why settle for Olive Oyl
when you could be Xena?

December 1

Time to LOL!

God, Godiva, and girlfriends—
what more do we need?

December 2

· ·

*The L*ord *is good;*
His lovingkindness is everlasting.

Psalm 100:5 nasb

December 3

If God is in control, closed doors aren't accidental. They're supposed to be closed. They're not an oversight that slid by when God sneezed. They're part of the plan.

December 4

· ·

Jesus, regardless of my appearance,
make me altogether lovely—like You.

December 5

We can't change every situation,
but through the Lord's power, we can
choose our responses to them. And that
makes the difference between victory and defeat.

December 6

When you cross deep rivers, I will
be with you, and you won't drown.
When you walk through fire,
you won't be burned or
scorched by the flames.

Isaiah 43:2 cev

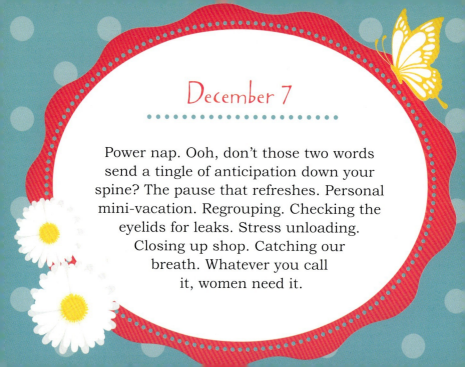

December 7

Power nap. Ooh, don't those two words send a tingle of anticipation down your spine? The pause that refreshes. Personal mini-vacation. Regrouping. Checking the eyelids for leaks. Stress unloading. Closing up shop. Catching our breath. Whatever you call it, women need it.

December 8

Just because I lose from time to time doesn't make me a *loser*. A Christlike attitude and demonstrating God's grace under fire determine who is a *winner*, not the score of a game.

December 9

Difficult people are often in our lives
for unseen purposes. God's purposes.
Perhaps to stretch us, grow us,
or sand down our sharp edges
by their friction. Remember,
even nutty lumps in the
batter add flavor!

December 10

I am surrounded by trouble,
but you protect me. . . .
With your own powerful
arm you keep me safe.

PSALM 138:7 CEV

December 11

Prayer is about understanding what Papa God wants for us.

December 12

Our heavenly Father is our true BFF.
He loves to hear our Twitter prayers—
those little snippets we can shoot
out at any time, day or night,
to keep us in constant
communication.

December 13

In the body of Christ, if we're hands,
we wish we were feet; if we're noses,
we'd rather be eyes. Sometimes we feel
like bunions. But God views us all as
equally important. Even us toenails.

December 14

*The Lord will hold your hand,
and if you stumble, you still won't fall.*

Psalm 37:24 cev

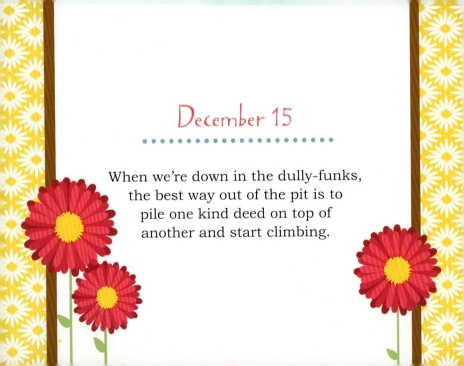

December 15

· · · · · · · · · · · · · · · · · ·

When we're down in the dully-funks,
the best way out of the pit is to
pile one kind deed on top of
another and start climbing.

December 16

It's incredible how much
difference a little optimism makes
in reducing everyday stress.
Everything looks surprisingly
brighter, warmer, more hopeful.

December 17

I am merely a rosebud;
Papa God is the Master Gardener.
It's only because of His water, fertilizer,
and loving care that I bloom and grow.

December 18

The Lord is good, a strong refuge when trouble comes. He is close to those who trust in him.

Nahum 1:7 nlt

December 19

....

Lord of all possibilities,
fill me with dreams. Big dreams.
Your dreams for me.

December 20

· · · · · · · · · · · · · · · ·

Didn't Jesus rebuke Martha
for her preoccupation as a human
do-ing rather than a human *be*-ing?

December 21

· ·

Master Encourager, help me
light up someone's life today—
to kindle their candle,
not blow it out.

December 22

Our LORD, we belong to you.
We tell you what worries us,
and you won't let us fall.

PSALM 55:22 CEV

December 23

· ·

Only God can turn
us downside up!

December 24

Creator of patience, fill my dry tank.
Remind me when I get frustrated
that it's me who has the problem.

December 25

. . . .

Papa God's cup of
forgiveness is bottomless.

December 26

· ·

"Here on earth you will have
many trials and sorrows.
But take heart, because
I have overcome the world."

JOHN 16:33 NLT

December 27

• •

Sometimes when we feel least
like doing something, it's the
very thing we need to do most.

December 28

Think about it: What were your top three worries this time last year? You're above average if you can remember more than one. What does that tell you about the transient nature of worrying?

December 29

Think about two areas of your life in which God has blessed you "far more abundantly beyond" your expectations. As we tread water in the stress-pool of life, we may not always *feel* blessed, but we definitely *are* blessed. Thank Him for His loving-kindness and provision.

December 30

• •

*God is a safe place to hide, ready to
help when we need him. We stand
fearless at the cliff-edge of doom,
courageous in seastorm and
earthquake, before the rush and
roar of oceans, the tremors
that shift mountains.*

PSALM 46:1 MSG

December 31

Peace is acquired by intentionally handing our heavenly Father our daily annoyances, dilemmas, and burdens one by one, minute by minute. By giving up the steering wheel, by making the choice to relax in the backseat, we can enjoy the journey and let Papa drive.